STRENGTH IN TIMES OF CRISIS

UNDERSTANDING HOW TO TURN YOUR CRISIS TO TESTIMONY

© Emeka Ejikeme

STRENGTH IN TIMES OF CRISIS

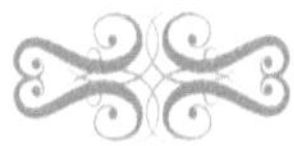

UNDERSTANDING HOW TO TURN YOUR CRISIS INTO TESTIMONY

REV. EMEKA EJIKEME

New York   Toronto   Maryland   Sidney

FOREWORD

I am excited to do a foreword to this book, STRENGHT IN TIMES OF CRISIS by a beloved servant of God and a son in the faith, so dear to my heart who has stood firm in his walk with God to the admiration of all.

The subject crisis in life, although one of the most widely taught in the school of management and social sciences in educational institutions is still one of which the church is largely ignorant about. While some undertake to attitude their lack of knowledge to fate others just see it as spiritually occurrences. Crisis management is a scare subject in our pulpits today, we try to give dry faith to everything that happens instead of applying biblical and Godly and Godly principles in handling crisis in life.

Crisis, like any other principle, must be learned, the book of James sheds a lot of light on this all important subject thereby justifies the writer of the book of Proverbs. What we need is a concise teaching on effective prayer and acquisition of wisdom. And this is what this book gives. A crisis is like the wind Jesus talks about that must blow to both houses; so is up to you to build yours solid.

Emeka Ejikeme himself is a man giving to Godly wisdom who has weathered so many crises and its chronicled in this book what has become his way of life, and the emblem of his ministry and which has worked for countless thousands. A young man who worked his way from zero to the top need to be listened to.

Greatly insightful and inspiring, I believe that its lucid language will appeal to you and teach you how to walk in wisdom in times of crisis in life. It's a masterpiece and must read.

Hon. Bishops Timothy

Ifedioranma Ph.D

■ TABLE OF CONTENT ■

STRENGTH IN TIMES OF CRISIS

UNDERSTANDING HOW TO TURN YOUR CRISIS TO TESTIMONY

Ⓒ Emeka Ejikeme

CHAPTER 1

Understanding A Crisis

We were under great pressure, far beyond our ability to endure, so that we despaired of life itself. 2 Cor. 1:8

No matter how hard things are right now, God is with you. No matter what is going on in your life now, God is completely aware of it and none of these things whether unpleasant or unbearable happen without God's knowledge.

A crisis is defined as a time of great pressure and difficulty, trouble, or danger beyond our ability to handle or endure; a time when things turn from better to worse. A crisis could be deemed as a dilemma; deadlock; trouble; problems or a very embarrassing situation. These conditions are associated with pain and distress.

You might be going through a crisis right now, you might be feeling all alone, and feeling like God does not care. These feelings are normal and are associated with crisis. That is what Apostle Paul was describing in this text.; He said in 2 Corinthians 1:8, 'we were under great pressure, far beyond our ability to endure'. A crisis can be so overwhelming but there is hope for us all.

We have all had the thought during our times of Crises how long Lord? How long do I have to bear this? Does God really care? 'I have prayed and fasted but there seems to be no help in view. Again, that is the way it sometimes feels during a crisis, yet God hears us, and He cares.

Crises are of an infinitely wide range. A crisis could be in marriage, job, or health. In any case, one thing is clear. It is a very unstable or crucial, in   which a decisive change is imminent; *especially*: one with the distinct possibility of a highly unpleasant outcome.

You might find it consoling that you are not an isolated case. Crisis time is like death, it has no respect for individuals – it comes to us all.

Even the great apostle Paul reported their great distress while in God's work.

We do not want you to be uninformed, brothers and sisters, about the troubles we experienced in the province of Asia. We were under great pressure, far beyond our ability to endure, so that we despaired of life itself. 2 Cor. 1:8

Whether you are the celebrated president of a nation or the pitiable peasant in the suburbs, crisis time is a sure thing. Though we don't all have the same crisis; our crisis may defer one from another but we all have a time crisis as a common denominator in our lives.

EXAMPLE OF CRISIS

Perhaps, you have received a terrible report from your doctor, it might even be a financial crisis with the possibility of losing your home or even family. It is possible that you have problems with your in-laws – whatever the situation happens to be, they are all considered crises. The relationship with your in law may have started out on the wrong foot. As time progressed it got increasingly worse and now is at a critical phase. It is a crisis- unless something happens to tilt the tide in another direction, this crisis might even lead to the collapse of your marriage.

Another crisis could be that your children are rebelling against you as a parent. They are threatening to leave home; their school attendance is nonexistent. You have employed every available means known to you to correct the situation to no avail. It is a crisis. You have threatened to disown them because of this crisis. Disowning your children, by the way, won't solve the problem. It is a crisis.

Whether you are the celebrated president of a nation or the pitiable peasant in the suburbs, crisis time is a sure thing.

Another man's crisis could even be as trivial as getting a speeding ticket, yet it is a crisis. And like all crisis, it is always a bad situation that turned worse over time because it is not handled in the right way or at the right time. When it's a crisis it takes away your peace and sleep. You are crying 'I don't deserve this' but you do because you failed to act. In other cases, the crisis is simply just too overwhelming for any one of us to handle, but praise God there is good news.

The good news is that crisis can be overcome. The key to overcoming crisis is first to learn to manage the crisis. In the following chapter, I will share with you how to manage crisis time.

■ ■

MANAGING CRISIS

Moses answered the people, "Do not be afraid. Stand firm and you will see the deliverance the LORD will bring you today. The Egyptians you see today you will never see again. [14] The LORD will fight for you; you need only to be still." Exodus 14:13-15 9 (NIV), other references: Exodus. 14:13-15, chap 5:20-23

The key to overcoming crises is to first understand how to manage them, We tend to want our problems to disappear by waving a magic wand. The Children of Israel were terrified as they were seemingly stuck between the dead end red sea and the furious Egyptian army. They cried, they cursed, they thought of stoning Moses. They were in despair. Just as the disciples of Jesus were when they were caught in a raging storm.

24 And they came to him, and awoke him, saying, Master, master, we perish. Then he arose and rebuked the wind and the raging of the water: and they ceased, and there was a calm. Luke 8:24

These are typically what people do in a crisis. But Glory to God! In the case of Moses, as was the case of Jesus disciples, the crisis was overcome by the power of God. You too can overcome your crisis. The first key is to change your paradigm; your outlook on problems. How do you see problems or crisis? How do you see yourself when you are overwhelmed? Do you think like a victim; like someone who is unfortunate or as a failure? It matters a lot how you see yourself and what you are going through.

YOUR WEAKNESS IS NOT A DISQUALIFICATION

Something that needs to be understood is that being weak is a sign that we have come to the end of our own strength. Being weak is a signal that we are humanly exhausted. 'I can't go much farther You don't help me' and that is when God steps in.

And the LORD said unto Moses, why do you cry unto me? speak unto the children of Israel, that they go forward: Exodus 14:15

This condition of weakness is not a penalizable offense. Rather, it gives God the permission to take His due place. When Moses faced this crisis, he cried to God. God did not blame him for being weak. The devil sometimes tells us that we are weak. So much so that we think we are the weakest of all men simply because we are facing a crisis.

If we do not experience these crises some of us may never experience the power of God in our lives. Human nature has shown us that when we feel we can handle a situation, we don't seem to need faith to do it. We are sufficient in our ability and have no need of faith in a situation like those. But wait until a condition far beyond our natural ability occurs then we become suddenly aware of our need for faith.

An example would be, the good car, assuming of course that we all have good cars, the car by which we commute to work every morning. All that is required is wake up humming songs getting into the car and off we go, we all seem to be serving God from this convenient corner. No sweat! But wait, one day trying to drive to work and the car won't start. Let's Suppose there is continuous difficulty every morning with the same car and the conclusion is that the car has–many issues but. There is no money to fix it and now the job is at stake. What to do becomes the preoccupation. Because now there is a crisis.

The sudden urge to speak in tongues wells up, and for some of us we do break out in tongues. We will find that every morning before getting into the car prayer and supplication goes up just for the car to take us to work and back because experience has taught us that the car does disappoint. You pray "Father I thank you, am going to work late, let this car start … "…. that is a prayer one might say when the need for prayer dawns.

> *If these crises don't happen to us, some of us may never experience the power of God in our lives*

recall the days when the car starts without problems; the battery was fine it started, and you hear the engine rev up- even under snow (the engine sounded good) it started without problems, then the thought or need for prayers wasn't evident. Faith wasn't applied but the day that the same car disappoints, one may think the lights were left on. The next day it disappoints again, and again the day after that. It is normal that when next any of us get into the car again we would with trepidation and will start praying before getting into the car 'In the name of Jesus .... power, power (speaking in tongues) … saying 'car you must not disappoint me today you must start…I speak to you immediately you must start……' Now we know we must pray. Alleluia!

It's a signal that man needs God when he has come to the end of himself. So, our weakness is not a disqualification- it is a signal to God indicating it is the time He takes over.

CRISIS IN LIFE ARE INEVITABLE

Crisis in life is inevitable. That includes the life of a Christian. Some Christians would say 'why me?' I say if not you, who would you suggest? No one can't run from it or shut themselves in a hole. Being holy or saintly does not exempt anyone from a crisis. That means as a Christian you should not expect to be exempt from a crisis.

The enemy will try to isolate you and whisper in your ear saying you are the only one going through a crisis. He would tell you it's because of your sin. The truth is that everybody goes through crisis regardless of whether they had sinned or not. You need to be ready to conquer and move on in your Christian life. Christianity is not an immunity to a crisis; nor a cancellation, denial, or blockade but there is a guarantee of victory after the crisis. People think when they are Christians they wouldn't go through a crisis that is incorrect, but there is a guarantee that you will come out of it victorious even as Jesus did.

CRISIS IS MEANT TO MAKE YOU STRONG

Crisis is meant to make one strong. It elevates you to another level through experiences the crisis provides.

My brethren, count it all joy when ye fall into divers temptations; Knowing this, that the trying of your faith worketh patience. But let patience have her perfect work, that ye may be perfect and entire, wanting nothing. James 1: 1-2

Crisis or problem, when well managed helps us stand tall and firm in our belief. Whenever you are challenged know this that the crisis has not come to hurt you but to build you up. Don't say 'why me' …it ought to be you because you want to be strong.

The management of crisis will always determine the result–Positive or negative. Crisis management will determine the outcome. Some Christians think God will protect them; that problems will not come their way. Crisis in marriage and job and children will always come, how you manage it determines the outcome. For example, in-laws may rise against you, how you manage the crisis will make your relationship with your in-laws better or worse

Crisis does not seem beneficial to anyone now, it is indeed grievous, or so it seems. It seems to have no benefit now but again I repeat for emphasis if managed well and with wisdom, it will turn into a blessing. It may feel sour today but it will be for your good tomorrow.

Even as a Pastor crisis will be experienced, but it toughens us up and makes the best Pastor out of us.

What makes one a good Pastor is how one manages a crisis. Parents may soon face serious situations with their children, i.e.–their children acting crazy. I have heard parents say they would disown their children. These are mere words and the situation may turn worse if not handled well.

> *The gift you have attracts crisis or problem. But when the crisis comes it provides you with the necessary training you need*

Some situations are not really crises but because of the way they were handled, they became crises. What is to one bread, may to another be a crisis.

Think of the twelve spies Moses sent up to spy on the promised land. Ten of the spies called it an insurmountable crisis but Joshua and Caleb called it 'bread'

...neither fear ye the people of the land; for they are
bread *for us: their defense is departed from them, and the*
LORD is with us: fear them not. Numbers 14:9

A perfect situation can therefore quickly deteriorate into a crisis if not properly handled. But if handled well it is not a crisis but bread!

CRISIS ARE CONSTANT VISITORS

Crises are constant visitors to men and women of great potential and bright futures. It really is a compliment to have a crisis. Crisis does not come to dead people. The more your potential the more problems you seem to have to attack.

Crisis comes with dual functions, it comes to take away from you and at the same time enrich you with experience.

So, in a crisis, you will see the interplay of both gift and experience come together to develop you.

The gift and experience matters. How you handle them determines the outcome you have. The gift you have will always attract crisis. Some people have the gift of gab as it is called. They are good with words but therein lies their problem. They can't seem to tame their tongue. Should they receive more training they would know how to handle their tongue. Many times, this training will come in form of a crisis. A crisis they entered because they misspoke or spoke when they weren't supposed to.

For example, some are very good dancers. They dance even while driving. They would dance while driving and misapply the break. And then they get into a serious mishap. But when they manage that gift of dancing properly the gift is a blessing.

> *A situation might be a crisis but the way you hand it might produce crisis and chaos...*

When these people learn through crises, not only are they safe they hone their gift and are enriched with wonderful experiences they can share with others.

Their experience is not what is or can be taught. The experiences they then share with us are real and rich.; as is said 'experience is the best teacher'.

When our gift does not receive proper training. chaos is inevitable. But after adequate training our gift blossoms. The management of the chaos determines our promotion.

Unfortunately, some never manage their chaos and they end up in jail or trouble.

It is not enough to confess positive and dream positive. You need to get training. Turn your crisis into training sessions. Alleluia! Get training because crises are inevitable.

For example, going to a theological school and going through the process of becoming a Pastor and being in ministry are two totally different things. We have seen people without theological training who came out as great Pastors and counselors because they went through due process. For example, the ability to deal with people is a training you cannot get in a seminary or theological school. It is very difficult for instance dealing with men particularly, most men don't like admitting they are wrong; Wise women will tell you that out of an experience that they have tried and have come to understand a man's pride. A pastor who has honed his gift can handle situations like these. So, it's not enough to know bible scriptures, the experience with people plus the bible knowledge will prepare one for real ministry.

Crisis grants you the experience that will create ways for promotion. Any potential you have which is your gift must pass through a time of chaos, or crisis and that is the time of your training.

ABILITY TO MANAGE DIFFICULT SITUATIONS

Crisis management gives you the ability to manage difficult situations. Though that you can effectively manage situations which are neither beneficial nor profitable.

Not only does the experience you gained through crisis help you manage your gifts it also helps you manage difficult situation in general.

For example, a man who is not just a Lawyer but had defended many clients with the same case as your case in court would give you a better advice than any intelligent lawyer without court experience. If you are looking for good advice, go to such Lawyer with good court experience. They can tell you things that other lawyers can't tell you because the case crisis has built in them a unique experience. He would sit you down and give you very good advice that would help you. Not all lawyers have the same experience.

It is good to go to school but those who do well, do more so because of experience.

You cannot avoid a crisis. Use the crisis to your advantage. In the next chapter, I will share with you some of the great benefits of crisis.

■ ■

BENEFITS OF PROPER CRISIS MANAGEMENT

For our light affliction, which is but for a moment, worketh for us a far more exceeding and eternal weight of glory; 2 Cor. 4:17

Managing crisis is the only way to defy a terrible situation and create something good out of it. When crises are well managed the benefits are immense. History will attest to the fact that crisis has produced most of the world's great leaders. Let's remember Joseph who was sold by his brothers and subsequently imprisoned. Through a crisis of thirteen years, he emerged as the prime minister of Egypt.

Abraham Lincoln story is very inspiring. It is a story of one crisis after another. But at the end of the day, we see what a distinctive President he became.
Abraham Lincoln was a businessman and as a businessman he failed. Not long after failing as a businessman he threw his hat into the political arena, failed there repeatedly. He lost his fiancée, had a nervous breakdown, but he eventually emerged victorious as one of the greatest leaders of our time and an icon, one known as Honest Abe.

Abraham Lincoln ran for Congress and was defeated. He ran a second time and again, was defeated. Then he ran for the Senate and lost. He ran for Vice President and lost. Lincoln ran again for the Senate and again was defeated.
Then, in 1860, Abraham Lincoln was elected President of the United States.

What matters most is not how many times you fail, but that you never stop trying or believing you can do it.

STEPPING STONE

Crises are stepping stones in disguise. *Moses answered the people, "Do not be afraid. Stand firm and you will see the deliverance the LORD will bring you today. The Egyptians you see today you will never see again. Exo. 14:13*

Israel kicked and squalled. They wanted to go back to Egypt because they were afraid. Moses essentially told them to use the crisis to their benefit, and they did. They crossed the red sea walking on dry land while the Egyptian army perished in the waters.

Through this crisis, there came a great divide between the nation of Israel and The Egyptians.

The Egyptians you see today you will never see again Ex. 14:13

The Red Sea was their crisis, but it is the same red sea that God used as the great deliverance tool for them. It is the red sea that permanently separated Israel from Egypt. Glory! Crises are stepping stones in disguise. It feels like an affliction, but it works for us an eternal weight of glory. What is an eternal weight of glory? That is a blessing.

My brethren, count it all joy when ye fall into divers temptations;

³ Knowing this, that the trying of your faith worketh patience James 1:2-3

So, shall it be for you in Jesus name! Every temptation will turn into a stepping stone for you.

VICTORIOUS

Joseph became the prime minister of Egypt after he was lied on and cast into prison. We say from prison to palace. Glory!

Imagine Joseph in that dungeon- dark and cold. He had no idea what was coming next. A light appeared in the tunnel when the butler whom he had helped was called back to pharaoh's palace. Joseph said

But think on me when it shall be well with thee, and shew kindness, I pray thee, unto me, and make mention of me unto Pharaoh, and bring me out of this house…Gen. 40:16

Yet did not the chief butler remember Joseph, but forgat him. Gen 40:23

The Butler forgot Joseph. The light that had appeared had disappeared just as quickly as it had appeared. But Joseph was no stranger to crisis, he continues to be the good and gentle Joseph who even in the dungeon and through each crisis never lost his gift.

If Joseph had killed himself, he would never have become prime minister. If he had lost his mind and started cursing at the prison warden he would never become king.

Managing crisis is the only way to defy a terrible situation and work out something good out of the crisis.

With the wisdom of God, you can use a crisis to achieve victory. It was through God's wisdom that Joseph handled his crisis well, and because of how well he managed it he was brought into the palace. Joseph was victorious.

Then Pharaoh sent and called Joseph, and they brought him hastily out of the dungeon: and he shaved himself, and changed his raiment, and came in unto Pharaoh. Ex. 41:14

Use your crisis to move from dungeon to palace. Don't be sorrowful. Be wise and strong use your crisis to catch up. It was in prison that Joseph learned to be king. That was where he developed his gift and learned people's skill. So, shall it be for you, such that when you look back you will be amazed where God has brought you! Then you will know you are victorious because of your crisis.

Consider it all joy, my brethren, when you encounter various trials, knowing that the testing of your faith produces endurance. And let endurance have its perfect result, so that you may be perfect and complete, lacking in nothing. James 1:2-4

In the next chapter, we will examine the tools to manage crisis and overcome a crisis.

■ ■

TOOLS IN OVERCOMING CRISIS

*Finally, be strong in the
Lord and in His mighty power. Eph 4:10*

There are certain virtues that must be in place if we must overcome in times of crisis. They are the elements of our faith. The good news is that through the work of Jesus on the cross we have all it takes to overcome. There are three main elements needed to overcome a crisis.

CONFIDENCE

One is Confidence. Confidence is like a propeller under a big ship which is not seen but it is what propels the ship. In a cargo ship, If the propeller breaks the ship doesn't move. Propellers cause them to sail. Confidence has the power to propel you during the storm of life. When there is no confidence a Christian naturally lacks the drive to move on in life. Confidence is something that tells you on the inside that whatever it is you are doing will work. Whether in your Marriage, immigration issues, though everybody is giving up but there is something in you that tells you it's going to work.

A professional might be telling you there is no way, but there is an inner witness cheering you on and insisting that you pay no attention to distractions. Confidence is like a propeller when you lose it, your ship will be stranded in the ocean. The devil wants to deflate your confidence.

So do not throw away your confidence; it holds a great reward. Heb. 10:35

Let your conversation be without covetousness; and be content with such things as ye have: for he hath said, I will never leave thee, nor forsake thee.

So that we may boldly say, The Lord is my helper, and I will not fear what man shall do unto me. Heb. 13:5,6

If one loses their confidence, they become stagnant. That is why we must build our confidence in God. It is confidence that makes one able to handle crisis and say I can be free from this problem. You don't run, you don't turn your back. Soldiers don't turn their backs to their enemy, the enemy might shoot. It is a sign of surrender to turn your back to the enemy. You can only defend yourself from the enemy's bullet if you are facing your enemy.

When David was fighting Goliath, the Bible talks about him running towards the giant.

As the Philistine moved closer to attack him, David ran quickly toward the battle line to meet him 1 Sam. 17:48

Confidence is a sustainer of God's promises. David knew the promises of God. He was confident in it. When we have the word of God that we are standing on and believing God for the manifestation in for example our marriages, we have confidence that our marriage will work, that the financial crisis we presently find ourselves in will be over and that although the doctors have told us it is impossible, but our God will fight for us. We know the word says no weapon fashioned against us shall prosper… therefore think to yourself although I have cancer it will not prosper in my body. Cancer is a weapon; it will not prosper. 'No sickness afflicting me will by any means hurt me.' They will come but will not hurt me. That is the sound of confidence.

So that we may boldly say, The Lord is my helper, and I will not fear what man shall do unto me. Heb. 13:5,6

Let us Build our confidence in the word of God so that when a crisis comes to us, we will stand on the word and soar like an eagle.

> *Confidence prepares a platform for you—it gives you a push, and sustains your spiritual stamina.*

Confidence prepares a platform for us —it gives us a push, and sustains our spiritual stamina. anyone can be skillful but without stamina; After a few minutes they are worn out. Think of confidence as spiritual stamina. For example, in a soccer game if in the first two minutes you score two goals but for the remaining 98 minutes, let's say you open your self to concede more goals because you have no stamina to continue. Confidence is spiritual stamina. When you are tired your confidence will pump you up. That is why and how we know that God is going to take us through.

RELIABILITY

O LORD, who may abide in Your tent… who keeps an oath even when it hurts, and does not change their mind; Psalm 15:4

Another is reliability. Everybody is looking for someone they can lean or rely on. Think of an employee who calls in late or is absent often. He is always giving one excuse or the other. 'oh, I am running late' or "I have a flat tire.' It seems like he is having a flat tire every day. And has been so for the last 3 days and now for the fourth day and the fourth time he is using the same excuse to call off work or come late, the company will not and cannot run on flat tires. Such a person will eventually be fired. He is not reliable.

Imagine if each time you chose or decide to come to church you must pray 'oh God please let my Pastor be in Church'. He is expected to be at church every Sunday. you know you will find him. You know the church doors are always open. That is reliability.

Reliability is the ability to fall back on something without exercising any fear or doubt. Just as you come to church without any fear that the church doors will be closed.

I pray that any confidence you have in God shall not be disappointed in Jesus name. Every crisis of the enemy that the enemy is using to bring you down is disappointed in Jesus name.

Being reliable or self-reliant may be discounted as not depending on God or rejecting His existence. That is not true.

Integrity matters during crisis, your character is put to test during crisis.

INNER STRENGTH

When I think of all this, I fall to my knees and pray to the Father, the Creator of everything in heaven and on earth. I pray that from his glorious, unlimited resources he will empower you with inner strength through his Spirit. Eph 3:14 (NLT)

The third virtue we must have to overcome crises is an inner strength. We have an inner man and this strength we are talking about comes from our spirit man. When people assess your weakness, they are basically referring to your mind or your physical body, but God refers to your inner man.

The spirit of man is the candle of the LORD, searching all the inward parts of the belly. Prov. 20:27

People may look at you outwardly and think what a weakling! What a banana! But in the spirit, you're a lion. Demons are afraid of you. If they dare come to harass you in the spiritual world you will and can dispose of and chase them away instead of them chasing after you. That is an inner strength. There are those who claim to be strong physically but are nothing in the spirit. God needs your inner strength to act, your inner strength comes in when naturally you are weak. The devil may come but what will he have the power to do?

There are people who have this terrible experience of being tied down in the dream. That is because they are weak when it comes to their inner strength. Upon waking up they would experience terrible symptoms. Build your inner strength. Alleluia!

For which cause we faint not; but though our outward man perish, yet the inward man is renewed day by day. 2 Cor. 4:16

But you say, 'Pastor how do I build my inner strength? How do I lay a foundation?' Building an inner strength is not a destination. It is a lifelong journey. In the next Chapter, I will focus on how to build inner strength.

■ ■

HOW TO BUILD YOUR INNER STRENGTH

But they that wait upon the LORD shall renew their strength; they shall mount up with wings as eagles; they shall run, and not be weary; and they shall walk, and not faint. Isa 40:31

As I said in the previous chapter building an inner strength is not a destination. It is a life Journey of faith. You cannot build your inner strength overnight any more than a boxer can build his muscles overnight. No man can say he is born strong, no one has ever arrived in life spiritually strong, nor will one ever, your inner strength must be built. When overcoming a crisis, building an inner strength is the most important. This is what separates winners from losers; victors from not so victorious and this is what decides the outcome of any crisis.

If a man's inner strength is weak he will fail miserably.

If thou faint in the day of adversity, thy strength is small. Prov. 24:10

Crisis can either crush you or carry you; will either cut you or cut for you. The deciding factor here is the inner force with which we go through the crisis. In building our strength, which is our inner force there are several important mindsets we must develop. We must undergo mental and spiritual changes; the bible talks about the renewal of our minds. Some of these renewals come at a great cost of comfort.

If we do not have the proper attitude and mindset we may lose courage and faint.

KNOW THAT BUILDING INNER STRENGTH IS A LIFE JOURNEY

Building one's strength is not a destination, it's a life-long journey, and explains why sometimes we are up, and

> *Building your inner strength is not a destination, it's a lifetime journey*

sometimes we're down, and it's throughout our lifetime. Sometimes we feel discouraged, sometimes we're tied up, sometimes we feel we don't want to go to church, and sometimes we can't wait until morning to go to church, it's natural.

Even as a Pastor I don't always feel like going to preach every Sunday. I feel the same reluctance you sometimes feel. But I come because I must; I am in a tight corner. That does not mean one is not spiritual or that one is a backslider. It is the weakness of the flesh.

Watch and pray, that ye enter not into temptation: the spirit indeed is willing, but the flesh is weak. Matt 26:41

The inner man must continually be exercised as the human muscle is exercised. That is why it's a continuous thing. You may have heard or seen athletes who every morning goes jogging. They have a regular schedule in the gym where they lift weights and do strenuous exercises that build various aspect of their bodies. After a very long time, you will notice that the athlete body is well defined by the training. You will see a well built, muscular athlete whose muscles have been developed from the routine exercises.

Everyone who lives on milk is still an infant, inexperienced in the message of righteousness. But solid food is for the mature, who by constant use have trained their sensibilities to distinguish good from evil. Hebrews 5:14

The scriptures say those *'who by constant training'*. Constant training, not of our bodies but of our inner man. This is the picture the apostle is painting here. We should not be discouraged by the baby steps we make every day. We may even fail sometimes but it only makes us better. It will not crush us. Usually, God will not allow us to go through any crisis that would destroy us.

No temptation has overtaken you except what is common to mankind. And God is faithful; he will not let you be tempted beyond what you can bear. But when you are tempted, he will also provide a way out so that you can endure it. 1 Cor 10:13

Crisis or temptation come in sizes. With every crisis, we overcome our strength is built up. There is no one final place in this journey where we can say absolutely we have arrived. There is no limit how far we can develop ourselves. Paul said to the Philippian Church I press toward the mark.

I press toward the mark for the prize of the high calling of God in Christ Jesus. Phil. 3:14

'Press' means exerting pressure. Moving forward with rigor. Making progress against resisting forces. It demonstrates to us that it is a journey to build our inner strength. Praise the Lord, building our strength is not an automatic destination, it's a journey, it's a lifelong journey, so when you feel down, don't remain down, Praise the lord.

Your Perspective on God

Your perspective on God is justified in your inner strength. Knowing God is the strength. It takes more than just attending church or merely reading the Bible to know God. There are depths that we need to tap into when it comes to knowing God.

For example, if you are seated at a corner of a very big building, and your eyes can decipher the height, weight, and depth of the building but would not be able to decipher what is inside. This is the kind of limited knowledge we have when it comes to God: we have a limited perspective when we are at the corner.

For as I walked around and examined your objects of worship, I even found an altar with the inscription: To an unknown God. Therefore what you worship as something unknown. Acts 17:23

Praise the lord, what I am trying to articulate is that our perspective of God is underlined by our inner strength. From which angle are you seeing God? Are you seeing God as only a disciplinarian; who comes only when we are wrong to correct?-How do you personally see God? Is He a merciful God to you? Do you see and know you have a God that can stand up for you and protect you whenever and anywhere you're in trouble?

Many of us do not see that about our God, we do not know that even when we are not right God is ready to save us.

Sometimes when we fail we are awfully hard on ourselves. Because we see God as a regular high court judge who is so strict and would stop at nothing to send us to the dungeon. But brothers and sisters God is love. He knows our weaknesses.

> *For he knows our frame; he remembers that we are dust. Psalm 103:14(ESV)*

God knows how much you can bear, He will never leave you. He also knows what each of us is going through and exactly how we feel. Even when you are failing God will not cast you out. It's important that we understand God from the perspective of love. He is love. He will never allow crises to crush us. He will always send a rescue team just in time.

> *No evil will befall you, nor will any plague come near your tent. For He will give His angels charge concerning you, To guard you in all your ways. They will bear you up in their hands. Psalm 91:11*

God is like a mother to us. What do you think can separate us from the love of our mothers? What do you think can make any mother abandon a child?

God is just like a mom, or a dad, and even more so. We as earthly parents, if our children get themselves in a jam we first make sure the child is out of trouble then we begin to scold the child. If You happen to see a car about to hit your child while he or she is crossing the street and you understand it's your child's, fault. No parent will just let the child go on without trying to either protect the child or stop the car by alerting the driver, in some cases, some parents will risk their lives in making sure their child is safe, and cannot and will not rest until the car has driven off and they have been able to ensure the life of the child.

But after the child is in safety you may yell, but you will first take the action to save the child and later give the scolding. That is a vivid picture of what God does.

For we do not have a high priest who is unable to empathize with our weaknesses, but we have one who has been tempted in every way, just as we are--yet he did not sin. Heb. 4:15

For I am persuaded, that neither death, nor life, nor angels, nor principalities, nor powers, nor things present, nor things to come, nor height, nor depth, nor any other creature, **shall** be able to **separate us from the love of God**, which is in Christ Jesus our Lord. Rom. 8:38,39

Unfortunately, some of us think that God will leave us when the chips are down especially when one is at fault and allow us to crash. That is not God. Alleluia! The understanding that God is a merciful God should help in building our inner strength giving us the right perspective about God. When we have lived with and waited on Him,–we will then understand the way He operates.

DIVINE ABILITY IN A PACK

Your inner strength is your divine ability in a pack. which means it's a latent energy stored away for you. The crisis you presently are going through continues to trump up energy for you.

For our light affliction, which is but for a moment, worketh for us a far more exceeding and eternal weight of glory; 2 Cor. 4:17

The afflictions work for you an eternal weight of glory. It works power for you. The word used here is *'weight of glory'*. When problems arise, you will be amazed what comes out of you. The power is available for use. If we never go through any troubles, we will never know what we have in us. Our potential is revealed when we are backed up

> **unfortunately, some of us think God will abandon us and allow us to crash when the chips are down especially when we are at fault. That is not true.**

into a corner. Then and only then will we do amazing things.

The divine ability in a pack. Don't forget that word 'packaged', so it's like electric energy stored up in a battery that you can use for your Flashlight, but when you leave unused it could get spoiled. It's like the battery in your car that that cranks your starter, move the crankshaft, and it sparks up the spark plugs, and then your engine revs up. Praise the lord! But unless you put the battery to use and make sure the–connections are well corrected, the car will not start.

We now understand that we have divine strength, that every believer has the divine strength that is toned by crises. This ability of God in you is very

> *We are not alone. Even the great Prophet Elijah had crisis*

powerful if only it can be put to work. When it is untapped you don't' know it's there until it is used. It's just like a gift that is given to you, it's only when it is opened and used that you can profit from the gift. Praise the Lord!

But we have this treasure in earthen vessels, that the excellency of the power may be of God, and not of us.
2 Cor. 4:7

There is power in every believer which is the Excellency of God. This power is augmented by the proper use of crisis. This power is like a power pack in us. Amen.

Understanding Satan's Strategy

We have to understand Satan' tactics during the time crisis. God attempts to use the crisis and Satan attempts to use it to his advantage as well. During the time of crisis, Satan comes around with an accusatory voice. A deafening defeating clatter constantly in our ears. He says, 'oh you cannot come of this' this is not like the other time. 'oh, you are completely screwed' worst of it he says, 'nobody cares'. This is the reason why people fail in the time of crisis. Yet these words are all lies.

If you give attention to Satan, he will give you instruction. His instruction is never accurate. He will make you resign from the fight and give up. Do not give up or give in. God is with you always.

and, lo, I am with you always, even unto the end of the world. Amen. Matt. 28:20

The truth is that when we go through crises we are in the company of great men and women. We are not alone. Even the great Prophet Elijah had a time crisis. In the next chapter, we will examine what crisis he went through and how he overcame.

■ ■

■ **CHAPTER 6** ■

LESSONS FROM ELIJAH'S CRISIS

Elijah was a man subject to like passions as we are…James 5:17a

What lessons can we learn from this great prophet? Indeed, he was a great man. He called fire from heaven a few times. He prayed and called for rain and it rained. He performed amazing miracles including raising the dead. Yet the Bible says he is just as weak as anyone of us.

Elijah was a man subject to like passions as we are…James 5:17a

So, when you're weak don't condemn yourself. When your natural strength ends that is when the strength of God starts in your life. Praise the Lord! If Elijah overcame we too can overcome, that is the point Apostle James is trying to make. 'Elijah was a man like us', yet he did great things. We can too. He was weak and demonstrated his weakness. But God came through for him. Let us glean some divine truths that will help us in times of crisis.

THE BIG MOUTH OF THE ENEMY

Now Ahab told Jezebel everything Elijah had done and how he had killed all the prophets with the sword. 2 So Jezebel sent a messenger to Elijah to say, "May the gods deal with me, be it ever so severely, if by this time tomorrow I do not make your life like that of one of them." 1 King 19; 1

When Jezebel heard that Elijah has slain prophets of Baal with fire. She became very furious. According to the text, she vowed to make Elijah's life more miserable than the prophets of Baal.

That is what I call the big mouth of the enemy, the enemy has a big mouth. He intimidates you by words, he speaks fear, he says you are finished; that you are literally done for, for you that is going through crisis at this moment, he could whisper in our ears something like 'watch it you are not going to make it' he continuously speaks these lies to us. Like Jezebel' ever so severely. I will deal with you'.

---

when you're weak don't condemn yourself. When your natural strength ends that is when the strength of God starts in your life

---

Another example can be a woman who is trying to have a child he would whisper in your ear and say 'you know, there is no possibility of you having children? 'Did you not hear what the Doctors said'. For some others suffering from cancer, he may say 'look at yourself you are done! The Doctor says you have three months to live the report is you have cancer. That is the voice of Jezebel. He might be telling you right now 'Oh, you will soon be poor, homeless, sick and alone.' These voices we hear speaking terror and fear is the voice of Jezebel trying to intimidate us.

And I heard a loud voice in heaven, saying: "Now have come the salvation and the power and the kingdom of

our God, and the authority of His Christ. For the accuser
of our brothers has been thrown down, he who
accuses them day and night before our God. Rev. 12:10

The devil is the accuser of the brethren. All he does is to accuse us in any way he could. When you hear that accusatory voice just know it is the enemy. The scripture says he is the accuser of our brothers. The devil has a loud mouth, he is the one that tells you that your husband has started acting weird-spreading stories of how dissatisfied and unhappy he is in the marriage and says, 'you will soon get a divorce letter….'

The devil likes to make stories up, the voice of Jezebel is the voice that destroys your inner man; your inner strength. And he speaks through Jezebel, back to prophet Elijah, the man of God; a man that God has used to bring fire down was terrified by that voice.

I am restless in my complaint and am surely
distracted, Because of the voice of the enemy, Because of
the pressure of the wicked; For they bring down trouble
upon   me   And   in   anger they   bear a
grudge against me. My heart is in anguish within me,

And the terrors of death have fallen upon me…Psalm 55:5

Do not allow anyone to discourage you. If you listen to the devil, you will be in torment. You will be on the run like Elijah. You will be restless and distracted.

There is no fear in love; but perfect love casteth out fear: because fear hath torment. He that feareth is not made perfect in love. 1 John 4:18

Do you feel discouraged? Our founding fathers were discouraged, but they didn't remain discouraged Alleluia! Are you down? Our founding fathers, the patriarchs were down once, but they didn't remain down for long. You are here today, you are discouraged, and your mind is cast down, you are asking yourself if there indeed is a God? Realize that it is not you only that is asking that question, even some prophets have asked that question. Imagine, Pastor's and prophets alike pray for people that are longing to be pregnant, while their own wives are at home barren. They pray for people to be prosperous, while they themselves live from hand to mouth. They pray for people to be healed but they carry sicknesses in their bodies. They have asked that question is there really a God?

'And then Jezebel sent a messenger unto Elijah, a messenger saying, so let God... let the gods do to me and more also if I make not thy life as the life of one of them by tomorrow about this time.'

About this time, the devil chooses the time wisely - so that he can intimidate you, he then laughs at you and says, "you will soon have problem", He leads you to fear, he wants to deflate your inner man; he wants you to die before the testimony comes. Voices are coming into your spirit, you're hearing them, they are speaking, even when you're driving it does not cease, those are the voices of Jezebel. Praise the lord we have the victory.

You Have Overcame Greater problems In The Past

And when he saw that, he arose, and went for his life, and came to Beersheba, which belongeth to Judah, and left his servant there.

Look at verse 3 above. This is the story of Elijah, a man God has used greatly, to bring fire down. As a matter of fact, this incident was happening shortly after God has used him to bring fire from heaven to destroy 450 Baal prophets, and now the voice of one woman is putting him to flight.

Discouragement is often devastating. Brethren what we always must remember is that there are great things we have done, in the past certain things God has helped us escape, that is far more challenging than the present things we are currently going through that has us so discouraged. Ask yourself this question seriously, where you are today? What is the small thing that has you so shaken up? Tell yourself, remind yourself that you have faced bigger things and you have succeeded. You did it, overcame it and went your way and this one is relatively small now. No need to shake like a vegetable!

Why are you in despair, O my soul? And why are you disturbed within me? Hope in God, for I shall again praise Him, Psalm 43:5

If you can cast your mind back, you will see that what you are going through today is small compared to what you have gone through in your life. If it is possible for you to place them side by side, you will see the truth, but the enemy magnifies the present problem to make sure you don't see your future or remember your past victories. Praise the Lord, alleluia.

Ye are of God, little children, and have overcome them: because greater is he that is in you, than he that is in the world. 1 John 4:4

Faith says you have already overcome. You are not trying to overcome. You have already overcome.

ANGELIC VISITATION

But he himself went a day's journey into the wilderness, and came and sat down under a juniper tree: and he requested for himself that he might die; and said, it is enough; now, O LORD, take away my life; for I am not better than my fathers. And as he lay and slept under a juniper tree, behold, then an angel touched him, and said unto him, Arise and eat.

Let us look at verse 5 together, the lord told him 'Arise and eat! Is God not wonderful? God knew he was discouraged and he brought him food. People have not been able to imagine a God like that. That is sensitivity and love.

Tell your yourself now, arise and eat. When the enemy voices get through to you. You lose appetite for food. People can tell by just observing the way some of us walk that we are going through something major now.

The bible says that Elijah made up his mind to die, the word' die' here means he has given up hope. You may be reading this book -you are ready to give up. I have good news for you, you're about to receive an angelic visitation, Alleluia!

An angelic visitation connotes solution when there is no solution, that is when angels visit. Alleluia, as you're reading this book, you may have already concluded your own case is different and in your case, this is really the end I'm finished, no! Listen to me brethren God is saying it's not finished. As a matter of fact, when you say it's finished God says that it is the beginning of your testimony. Praise the lord. Think about Hagar – Sarah's maid - alone in the wilderness. She and Ishmael were completely alone in the middle of nowhere, but God came through.

And Abraham rose up early in the morning, and took bread, and a bottle of water, and gave it unto Hagar, putting it on her shoulder, and the child, and sent her away: and she departed, and wandered in the wilderness of Beersheba.

15 And the water was spent in the bottle, and she cast the child under one of the shrubs.

16 And she went, and sat her down over against him a good way off, as it were a bow shot: for she said, let me not see the death of the child. And she sat over against him, and lift up her voice, and wept.

17 And God heard the voice of the lad; and the angel of God called to Hagar out of heaven, and said unto her, what aileth thee, Hagar? fear not; for God hath heard the voice of the lad where he is.

18 Arise, lift up the lad, and hold him in thine hand; for I will make him a great nation.

19 And God opened her eyes, and she saw a well of water; and she went, and filled the bottle with water, and gave the lad drink. Gen. 21: 14-19

God will come through for you when all else fails. Hagar was afraid. She had given up. She believed that there is no hope for her child. But God came through by sending an angel. Be ready for an angelic visitation. We also read of Gideon in the book of judges. How he threshed wheat in a wine press, Hiding from the Midianites, Hopeless and insecure. But God sent an angel.

The angel of the LORD came and sat down under the oak tree at Ophrah that belonged to Joash, ·one of the Abiezrite people Gideon, Joash's son, was ·separating some wheat from the chaff in a winepress to keep the wheat from the Midianites 12 *The angel of the LORD appeared to Gideon and said, "The LORD is with you, ·mighty [courageous] warrior!"*

13 *Then Gideon said, " ·Sir, if the LORD is with us, why ·are we having so much trouble, why has all this happened to us? Where are the ·miracles [wonderful deeds] our ancestors told us about? They said, "Didn't the LORD bring us up out of Egypt? But now the LORD has ·left [abandoned] us and has ·handed us over to the Midianites."*

14 *The LORD turned to Gideon and said, "Go with your strength and ·save Israel from the ·Midianites ·I am the one who is sending you. "*

15 *But Gideon answered, "Lord, how can I ·save Israel? My ·family group is the weakest in Manasseh, and I am the ·least important member of my family."*

16 *The LORD answered him, "I will be with you. ·It will seem as if the Midianites you are fighting are only one man "*

Gideon was threshing wheat in a wine press. He was hiding from the Midianites. You don't thresh wheat in a wine press. But that was the only way he could hide from the brutality of the Midianites. Gideon also said that

But now the LORD has left [abandoned] us and has handed us over to the Midianites…

Gideon had given up hope. He even believed the Lord has abandoned Israel. Do you feel abandoned? Like your prayers are not been answered? You are in good company. The company of people like Gideon. As God came through for Gideon so will he come through for you In Jesus name!

God said a shocking thing to Gideon in verse 14. He said Gideon is a man of valor. Oh, my!

"The LORD turned to Gideon and said, "Go with your strength and save Israel from the Midianites I am the one who is sending you. "

You may think you are weak because you are hiding. Because you are constantly harassed by your creditors. Yet God says go in this your strength. You have strength brothers and sisters. Praise God!

School of Experience

Back to our main text. Learning from Elijah. God baked cake for Elijah.

And he looked, and, behold, there was a cake baken on the coals, ….1 Kings 19:6

It takes the experience of crisis to excel in time of challenges. God allows you to go through certain things because of your future responsibilities. There are lessons, you must learn now that will equip you to properly manage the success of your future.

God allowed you to go through certain horrible experiences in life for this purpose. What you learn from what you are going through today will help you in the future. All the experience you have gathered which you may call suffering, it is not suffering but the school of life experience.

You are crying 'the suffering is too much' and God says 'ok, but learn your lessons for now, I'm going to give you an assignment, what you learn today will help you tomorrow'. Alleluia!

The things, the devil is using to torment you today, God will use the experience to give you victory. Alleluia.

And he looked, and, behold, there was a cake baked on the coals, and a cruse of water at his head. And he did eat and drink, and laid him down again

Why did the bible mention the word 'coal' The bible could have just said, and he saw cake? Why coal? The word coal there is reminding the prophet of process, experience, and the things God has done. You know it's easy to see challenges and back off without remembering that God has brought you out of challenges more difficult than what you are currently going through today. Say out loud to yourself 'I will arise and eat!'

PREPARE FOR THE LONG JOURNEY

Let us examine Elijah's crisis even further. God told him to eat because his journey is great.

And the angel of the LORD came again the second time, and touched him, and said, Arise and eat; because the journey is too great for thee 1 King 19:7

The journey is too far for you, you know sometimes you get weak. You can't even comprehend what is in front of you. You don't know this, but your journey has yet to start. If you are giving up now do you know what greater challenge may lie in front of

> **God allowed you to go through certain horrible experiences in life for this purpose. What you learn from what you are going through today will help you in the future**

you?

What you will see later in life could be greater than anything you have ever seen. In fact, it makes your current experience look like a joke.

Do not die before your great testimony comes. You learn from the experience and continue.

When a child is growing up it is quite an experience, getting married is an experience but raising kids, is another experience altogether. In every point of life where ever you are there are challenges, that is why the phrase *'every level has a devil'*, was coined. It's not saying that every level has devils necessarily, but that in every level you are, there are devils looking for you because of your level. There are levels of temptations you will experience because you are a parent, that people who are not parents don't know or understand.

There are temptations you contend with basically because you have a husband. Those that are unmarried could care less. They can go out and come back home anytime they desire. Unfortunately for my married sisters going out and coming in at whatever time you desire is out of the question. You will have your husband calling, asking where you are and what you were doing. And at times demanding you drop whatever doing and come home at that moment.

The same demands are of married men as well, when unmarried, things like sleeping over at a friend's home and from there go to work was okay but when married such liberties are done away with.

Again, I repeat there are certain things you go through in life because of your level or station in life. Every level has their own devils. That's why going back to our story, Elijah was touched and told to eat. Your journey is too far, fill your belly well and drink a lot of water. Stop shaking like a leaf.

"If you have raced with men on foot and they have worn you out, how can you compete with horses? If you stumble in safe country, how will you manage in the thickets by the Jordan? Jer. 12:5

God asked Elijah to eat so he can have more strength for the fight that lay ahead. If we faint because of Jezebel, how can we succeed in the bigger fight that lay ahead?

We don't usually know what God has in store for our lives, therefore, we continue to fight for we refuse to die before our time? Come on, brethren let's wake up there! Fill our bellies with food because our journey is indeed far… tell yourself 'my journey is too far'. Some of us are giving up, we are in the process of surrendering thinking our lives are over, it's time for us to shake ourselves and Wake up to eat!

Some of us our children are still young, and we complain about the challenges raising them, we forget that they will grow up, they will have children of their own, then there will be the challenge of being a grandparent, and God willing a great-grandparent. When children, some grown and not so young will come into your house with all manner of issues day and night not giving you the time to sleep, as it is with some of our older saints in our midst what would you say?

The challenge of dealing with children coming from different parents of diverse backgrounds, all with their own behaviors and values coming into your house. Imagine!

As a parent you all know how you dealt with your immediate children in your house, you know them, and could predict with some level of accuracy where their behaviors stem from, but as a grandparent or great-grandparent your influence is lessened, you are sometimes at a loss as to what precipitated a certain reaction.

You do not know that diversity can be quite difficult to deal with. And you as a grandparent you are obliged to treat them alike and make them happy. That is a different level in life. Praise the lord.

So, when God speaks arise for your journey is still far, do not give up. Don't kill yourself because you have had some disappointments. Stay focused.

Finally, be strong in the
Lord and in His mighty power. Eph. 6:10

You still have a life to live. Don't kill yourself because you lost a job. You don't want to destroy yourself because you missed out on anything; you still have many opportunities in life. And God is speaking to you today 'arise for your journey is still far. Alleluia, praise the Lord!

RENEWED STRENGTH

What happened to Elijah next was amazing. Elijah was so much invigorated that he went in power and might forty days and forty nights, that is 960 hours nonstop without another meal. Let us read verse 8 and 9,

And he arose, and did eat and drink and went in the strength of that meat forty days and forty nights to Horeb the mount of God. And he came thither unto a cave, and lodged there; and, behold, the word of the LORD came to him, and he said unto him, What doest thou here, Elijah?

Praise the Lord this was a man who had given up with serious suicidal thoughts. This was a man who thought everything has ended for him. This was a man who thought 'O ... because this happened to me I am done.' I don't know where you are today, maybe you have a problem in your family, you think there is no hope, maybe your job is shaking you think there is no way, maybe something has happened to your health you think there is no hope, maybe you have a need, or heard some bad news concerning your parents, and you think there is no hope, I command in Jesus name , no matter the news you have heard, no matter the story you have heard, no matter the complaint you have heard, receive strength for your journey, for God is on your side.

My flesh and my heart may fail, but God is the strength of my heart and my portion forever. Psalm 73:26

I can do all this through him who gives me strength. Philippians 4:13 NIV

He gives strength to the weary and increases the power of the weak. Isaiah 40:29 NIV

The same man that wanted to die now has walked for forty days and forty nights, with just one meal, Alleluia. That is the strength of God, a man who gave up, this same person has taken a journey for forty days and forty nights. Do you know what it means to walk for forty days and forty nights? This man was hiding himself for fear thinking there is no more hope. Perhaps, that's where you are now; hiding yourself; you've entered your cocoon, but

God is saying this today, 'come out of that place', you may have secluded yourself in your mind saying there is no way, you have told yourself this

---

The plan of the enemy is to get you downcasted, his plan is to make sure you don't make it, do not allow him!

---

is your last stop. I have good news for you, no matter where the enemy has kept you, wake up and move. When you think you are weak that is when His strength is made perfect, God is with you. Listen to the words of the great Apostle Paul

That is why, for Christ's sake, I delight in weaknesses, in insults, in hardships, in persecutions, in difficulties. For when I am weak, then I am strong.
2 Corinthians 12:10

The plan of the enemy is to get you downcast; his plan is to make sure you don't make it, his plan is to make sure your ministry ends, his plan is to make sure your marriage is destroyed. His plan is to make sure he shows you the reason why you must not live to see tomorrow. But I have good news for you, your journey is still far. God gives you an inner strength when you understand that He still has something great for you in the future, and it is quite discouraging when you look at the future and the future is dark. Praise the lord, receive an inner strength and understand that God still believes in you, there's a way for you, and He's making a way even if it seems there is no way for you now.

Elijah decided to himself that 'although God has used me to do great things, but this time I can't make it.' Just as you might think 'though God helped me when I was pregnant, but this time I can't make it,' or you could be thinking "though He gave me a husband when I needed one, but this time I can't make it." Or yours could be 'Though he healed me when I was sick, even when the doctors gave up on me and said I wouldn't survive, but this time I can't make it.' Better yet, what of this thought "Though He gave me a job and when I wasn't even expecting it, He gave me a better one, but this time I can't make it." "Oh, He opened doors of favor for me when all I was encountering were impossibilities but this time there's no way; there is no hope'. It is very easy to forget where you started, it's easy to forget what you have gone through in life. It's easy to forget all the testimonies God gave you in the past. Let me close this chapter with this scripture.

A Psalm of David. Bless the LORD, O my soul, And all that is within me, bless His holy name. 2Bless the

*LORD, O my soul, And forget none of His
benefits;…Psalm 103:1,2*

What is it that made Elijah have this special
presence of God in times of Crisis? In the next
chapter, we will learn the secret.

■ ■

■　C H A P T E R 7　■

WALKING WITH GOD IN TIME OF CRISIS

"Samuel took a stone and set it up between Mizpah and Shen. He named it Ebenezer, saying, 'Thus far the LORD has helped us'(I Sam. 7: 12).

Elijah enjoyed the help of God. You too can enjoy the help of God. Israel enjoyed this kind of help too. Israel's victory over the Philistines was decisive. Several cities the Philistines had captured were restored to Israel, and it was a long time before the Philistines tried to invade Israel again. To commemorate the divine victory, "Samuel took a stone and set it up between Mizpah and Shen. He named it Ebenezer, saying, 'Thus far the LORD has helped us'"

Ebenezer means "stone of help." but today brethren I want to declare that El Shaddai's name is Ebenezer, when you give up, He will step in. Before you give up my God will step in. Before you surrender my God will step in. Before you collapse my God will step in, I said before your discouragement, He will encourage you. Alleluia!

What are the factors that helped Elijah enjoy the presence of God in his time of crisis, so much so that God baked food for him and encourage him in almost like a face to face encounter? Here are some thoughts:

HAVE A RIGHT STANDING WITH GOD

Have the right standing with God. Elijah could have that encounter because he had a right standing with God. The right standing with God gives you right answers at the right point. God doesn't waste time on you when your ears are blocked ears. There are people and am sure we can all relate that no matter what advice they are given or how much help they get they are headed straight into problems,

---

I tell people not to be moved by emotion nor sentiment. That is not the quality of a leader

---

unfortunately, the same can be said for some of us no matter what God says we are going headlong into difficult situations. Some of us are curious, I dare say adventure freaks, but there is an old saying that is so apropos and that is curiosity killed the cat. No matter how much God warns people tend to do what they want to do. They cannot seem to differentiate between emotion and the right decision.

Remember Cain and Abel's story. Cain was angry at his brother. He let his feeling overtake his reasoning. He killed his brother. Before he killed his brother, God warned him.

but for Cain and for his offering He had no regard. So, Cain became very angry and his countenance fell. Then the LORD said to Cain, "Why are you angry? And why has your countenance fallen? "If you do well, will not your countenance be lifted up? And if you do not do well, sin is crouching at the door; and its desire is for you…Gen. 4:6,7

despite the warning of God, he went ahead and killed his brother Abel.

… when they were in the field, that Cain rose up against Abel his brother, and slew him.

And the Lord said unto Cain, where is Abel thy brother? And he said, I know not: Am I my brother's keeper?

And he said, what hast thou done? the voice of thy brother's blood cried unto me from the ground.

Gen. 4:8-10

Not having the right standing with God led to such a devastating consequence.

And now art thou cursed from the earth, which hath opened her mouth to receive thy brother's blood from thy hand; Gen. 4:11

I say this often and repeat it in the ears of everyone that will listen, do not to be moved by emotion or sentiment. That is not the quality of a good leader you only move by what God wants at that time.

This is true in all cases in life including parenting. A young girl had an accident when she was a toddler, and lost one of her eyes, and this is a true story the girl asked her mother what happened to her eyes. The mother answered her and said 'one day you took hold of a sharp object, I tried to take it out of your hand. I took it from you several times, but you cried each time for the object. I let you have and

Satan uses this voice to destroy your inner strength by accusation.

play with it just to comfort you and keep you from crying. The next thing I know I heard you crying this time in pain, I turned to find you bleeding through one of your eyes. To shorten the story dear that is how you lost your sight'

That right there was a decision the mother made from emotion and it cost her little girl her eye. There are Certain decision you will have to make these days for your children out of your will and stand on it, stick to it. Don't be carried away by emotion, theirs or yours.

There are certain decisions you must make for and concerning your partner right now, and you cannot allow your feelings to have the upper hand.
That was why when God stepped into the life of Elijah He said, 'now move'. Have a right standing with God. Everyone that wants to hear…that wants to move in the faith, to move in the strength of God, you must be a person that will stand with God. Praise the Lord!

RIGHTEOUSNESS EXALTS A NATION

Another secret of walking with God in the time of crisis is righteousness. The bible says in Proverbs 14:34,

Righteousness exalteth a nation: but sin is a reproach

Do you know what sin does? The devil uses sin to break your belief. Sin comes with condemnation. Sin has a voice that speaks, just as Jezebel's it condemns. It will tell you that you cannot achieve, attain because of some secret sin. This condemning voice causes you to be weak. Satan uses this voice to destroy your inner strength by accusation. That is why the bible made it clear in Rom. 8:1;

There is therefore now (there is now) no condemnation to them which are in Christ Jesus, …

Self-condemnation! when you want to be strong, more so, when you need to be strong the enemy will remind you of your secret. it will bring back to your remembrance everything you're hiding from others and perhaps yourself and will threaten exposure, and causes one to remain in a weak state.

Elijah was not zealous for worldly pleasure. Elijah was a holy man. He was having conversations with God and he had the audacity to say before God that He [Elijah] was zealous for God.

Then he came there to a cave and lodged there, and behold, the word of the LORD came to him, and He said to him, "What are you doing here, Elijah?" He said, <u>"I have been very zealous for the LORD, the God of hosts; for the sons of Israel have forsaken Your covenant, torn down Your altars and killed Your prophets with the sword.</u> And I alone am left; and they seek my life, to take away. "So, He said, "Go forth and stand on the mountain before the LORD."

This man was zealous for God. Imagine! What is the average believer zealous for today? Cars, Houses, expensive vacation and other base things. Elijah was zealous for God.

Elijah was in anguish because people no longer respect God and Israel had gone after idols.

Israel has Your covenant, torn down Your altars…Verse 10b

Today, we are indifferent to the cause of God. This man shares the same concerns with God. He was angry because of the filth in Israel. That is why and how he got God's attention.

We see sinners and we don't cry for them. We pass by them daily and don't remember or think that the person is damned. Some of even envy them, we could care less about their spiritual state but praise God It's not too late we can repent and immediately secure the presence of God. Alleluia!

The bible says if we sin, we have an advocate.

My little children, these things write I unto you, that ye sin not. And if any man sin, we have an advocate with the Father, Jesus Christ the righteous:

2 And he is the propitiation for our sins: and not for ours only, but also for the sins of the whole world. 1 John 2:1-2

God is very forgiving. He wants to walk with us. But He must cleanse us first from our sins.

If we say that we have fellowship with him, and walk in darkness, we lie, and do not the truth:

7 But if we walk in the light, as he is in the light, we have fellowship one with another, and the blood of Jesus Christ his Son cleanseth us from all sin. 1 John 1:6,7

But that is one of the secrets of Elijah. He was a righteous man. He was zealous for the things of God. That is why God used him powerfully.

THE WORD

The word of God so much encourages us. When we hear the testimony of the things God has done our inner strength is strengthened even more. The word of God helps us stand strong so that when we look at ourselves after walking with God for a while we find we are unshaken because God has spoken and it's very clear to us. Alleluia!

God revealed to us how in Deuteronomy 33:25 He will give us shoes of Brass and of Iron.

Thy shoes shall be iron and brass; and as thy days, so shall thy strength be.

You know what it means for God to give you shoes made of Iron and Brass?

Brass looks like gold, but it is not gold. Iron signifies strength, and then brass signifies glory and attraction.

Imagine you wearing shoes of Iron and brass in the spirit; the devil can't get away. it is not by our strength alone nor by, your power, but by the mercy of God. Alleluia! So, the word of God gives you the strength. John 10:35 says that,

If he called them gods, unto whom the word of God came, and the scripture cannot be broken;

It makes no difference to God whether those against you are many or few.

The word of God takes you from ordinary to extraordinary. The clarification of the word of God gets you an answer, when you need an answer. Apostle Paul says that I am lifted by the word of God, I was lifted by revelation and I saw, Galatians 2:2, I went up by revelation. There are certain answers that are not in your hands, but they are seen in the word of God. So, if you are a man or a woman of the word, you come out and listen to the word just as today, for God is speaking, an answer will always be readily available when there is trouble.

The word of God you know determines your worth in the spirit.

That was why when the devil came to tempt Jesus Christ. He started with the word, he says 'you are hungry, he says to him' turn the stone to bread'. Every temptation with which he tempted Jesus was through the word.

The enemy will always weigh you by what you know in the word. Not what you read, some people have read and become 'red.'

If you're weak it's a qualifier for God to come down. By your natural strength, you can't prevail. It says He will keep the feet of the saints …, He will guide your feet, He will strengthen your feet. Your *feet* signify your strength, it signifies your stand, where are you standing, He will keep you so that you will not slip off. And the wicked? He will deal with them, and then he concluded by strength shall no man prevail.

"He keeps the feet of His godly ones, But the wicked ones are silenced in darkness; For not by might shall a man prevail. 1 Sam. 2:9

He who says he is strong, he who thinks he stands let him take head least he falls.

So the one who thinks he is standing firm should be careful not to fall. 1 Cor.10:12

And that means when you are weak, it's a sign to say, God, I can't do it but you can do it for me. Alleluia!

God is speaking expressly. God has spoken that He's going to stand for you, He's going to act on your behalf, but God is making a demand today. Stand let your relationship with God be scared. God cannot be mocked, you can't mock God, God knows the intent of the heart, He knows the motive behind every action. What is your motive? What is our motives? Are they to scatter the church of Christ or

---

Judge your motive. What will I gain, let's forget this thing lets us... what will you gain?

---

to keep it holy and strong and together? what is our motive? Are they to improve...and encourage the man of God or to discourage Him? What are our motive? What will be the gain if the church scatters?

What will you personally gain? Really if the Church door closes? What would any of us gain?

Judge your motive. Continuously judge yourself, God is speaking expressly, underline everything you're doing by the word simple, he that sows shall reap. He that bless shall be blessed.

The bible even says when God is punishing our enemies, we should not laugh, if we do He will turn the punishment unto us. Can you imagine, but that is exactly what the bible says, don't even laugh.

Rejoice not when thine enemy falleth, and let not thine heart be glad when he stumbleth:

Lest the LORD see it, and it displeases him, and he turns away his wrath from him. Prov. 24:17,18

We are not allowed to say, 'I warned them, and this serves them right, nobody touches me and goes free'. God says not to say that now God is warning us 'if we continue to say things like that whatever suffering, they are going through God himself will turn it around and allow it to come on us. This is so, we dare not brag nor for a second dare to believe that's it's by our own power. Our actions should always be guided by the word, the word of God is a lamp, a lamp unto our feet, that before we take a step we should ask ourselves the question, what will God do? Praise the Lord, Alleluia.

DEPENDENCY ON GOD

Another secret in walking with God in time of crisis is the dependency on God. God is speaking expressly that we must depend on Him. And that our dependency on God is clearly based on the truth that God is a good God.

You may read 2 Samuel 10 verses 1-19. How the Ammonites hire armies to fight against Israel. But Israel depended on God. And God slaughtered all the armies.

… Thinkest thou that David doth honour thy father, that he hath sent comforters unto thee? hath not David rather sent his servants unto thee, to search the city, and to spy it out, and to overthrow it?

⁴ Wherefore Hanun took David's servants, and shaved off the one half of their beards, and cut off their garments in the middle, even to their buttocks, and sent them away….

⁶ And when the children of Ammon saw that they stank before David, the children of Ammon sent and hired the Syrians of Bethrehob and the Syrians of Zoba, twenty thousand footmen, and of king Maacah a thousand men, and of Ishtob twelve thousand men….

⁹ When Joab saw that the front of the battle was against him before and behind, he chose of all the choice men of Israel, and put them in array against the Syrians:

¹⁰ And the rest of the people he delivered into the hand of Abishai his brother, that he might put them in array against the children of Ammon.

¹¹ And he said, If the Syrians be too strong for me, then thou shalt help me: but if the children of Ammon be too strong for thee, then I will come and help thee.

¹² Be of good courage, and let us play the men for our people, and for the cities of our God: and the LORD do that which seemeth him good……

·¹⁹ And when all the kings that were servants to Hadarezer saw that they were smitten before Israel, they made peace with Israel, and served them. So, the Syrians feared to help the children of Ammon any more.

Because they depended on God, God slew an army from five nations by the hands of few soldiers of Israel. It's amazing what dependence on God can do. Glory to God.

The bible says that Joab was surrounded before and behind, from all corners. Read verse 9 again;

9 When Joab saw that the front of the battle was against him before and behind, he chose of all the choice men of Israel, and put them in array against the Syrians:

Are you backed up in the corner? Do you feel overwhelmed in your crisis? God will fight for you if you depend on him. It makes no difference to God whether those against you are many or few. He will defeat all that comes against you however formidable they are.

5 I depend on God alone; I put my hope in him.

6 He alone protects and saves me; he is my defender, and I shall never be defeated.

7 My salvation and honor depend on God; he is my strong protector; he is my shelter.

8 Trust in God always, my brethren. Tell Him all your troubles, for He is our refuge.

9Human beings are all like a puff of breath; great and small alike are worthless. Put them on the scales, and they weigh nothing; they are lighter than a mere breath.

10 Don't put your trust in violence; don't hope to gain anything by robbery; even if your riches increase, don't depend on them.

11 More than once I have heard God say that power belongs to Him

12 and that his love is constant. You yourself, O Lord, reward everyone according to their deeds. Psalm 62: 5-12

Praise God! I believe that strength is returning to you. In the next chapter, I will give you some scriptures that will help you in times of crisis.

■ ■

CHAPTER 8

ENCOURAGING SCRIPTURES AND PRAYERS IN TIME OF CRISIS

The adversaries of the LORD shall be broken to pieces; out of heaven shall he thunder upon them: the LORD shall judge the ends of the earth; and he shall give strength unto his king, and exalt the horn of his anointed. 1 Samuel 2:10 (KJV)

There are the closing thoughts of God concerning you and your enemies. He breaks your enemies in pieces, the adversaries of the lord shall be broken to pieces. Out of heaven shall heap thunder against them.

Sometimes it is difficult to hear God in your in your crisis. It is difficult to feel his presence at times. Feelings will deceive us, what we see could derail us., but God's word is ever true. Anyone that is an adversary to you is an adversary to God. When the early Church was going through the time of crisis. Jesus appeared to Paul

When he did he never asked why was Paul persecuting the Church. He asked why was Paul persecuting him [Jesus].

3 And as he journeyed, he came near Damascus: and suddenly there shined round about him a light from heaven:

4 And he fell to the earth, and heard a voice saying unto him, Saul, Saul, why persecutest thou me? Acts 9:3,4

The same Paul who caused much crisis became the great consortium to the Church.

Here are some scriptures that could help you in times of crisis.

SCRIPTURES IN TIMES OF CRISIS

1. *The adversaries of the LORD shall be broken to pieces; out of heaven shall he thunder upon them: the LORD shall judge the ends of the earth; and he shall give strength unto his king, and exalt the horn of his anointed. 1 Samuel 2:10 (KJV)*

2. *So, do not fear, for I am with you;*
do not be dismayed, for I am your God.
I will strengthen you and help you;
I will uphold you with my righteous right hand.
Isaiah 41:10 | NIV |

3. *But those who hope in the Lord*
will renew their strength.
They will soar on wings like eagles;
they will run and not grow weary,
they will walk and not be faint.
Isaiah 40:31 | NIV |

4. *My flesh and my heart may fail,*
but God is the strength of my heart
and my portion forever.
Psalm 73:26 | NIV |

5. *I can do all this through him who gives me
    strength. Philippians 4:13 | NIV |*

6. *He gives strength to the weary
    and increases the power of the weak.
    Isaiah 40:29 | NIV |*
7. *That is why, for Christ's sake, I delight in
    weaknesses, in insults, in hardships, in
    persecutions, in difficulties. For when I am weak,
    then I am strong.
    2 Corinthians 12:10 | NIV |*

8. *For the Spirit God gave us does not make us timid,
    but gives us power, love and self-discipline.
    2 Timothy 1:7 | NIV |*

9. *But the Lord is faithful, and he will strengthen
    you and protect you from the evil one.
    2 Thessalonians 3:3 | NIV |*

10. *Look to the Lord and his strength;
    seek his face always.
    1 Chronicles 16:11 | NIV |*

11. *I love you, Lord, my strength.
    The Lord is my rock, my fortress, and my
    deliverer;*

*my God is my rock, in whom I take refuge,
my shield and the horn of my salvation, my
stronghold.
Psalm 18:1-2 | NIV |*

12. *But I will sing of your strength,
in the morning I will sing of your love;
for you are my fortress,
my refuge in times of trouble.
Psalm 59:16 | NIV |*

13. *Be on your guard; stand firm in the faith; be
courageous; be strong.
1 Corinthians 16:13 | NIV |*

14. *Ah, Sovereign Lord, you have made the heavens
and the earth by your great power and
outstretched arm. Nothing is too hard for you.
Jeremiah 32:17 | NIV |*

15. *The Sovereign Lord is my strength;
he makes my feet like the feet of a deer,
he enables me to tread on the heights.
Habakkuk 3:19 | NIV |*

16. *For the word of God is alive and active. Sharper
than any double-edged sword, it penetrates even to*

dividing soul and spirit, joints and marrow; it judges the thoughts and attitudes of the heart. Hebrews 4:12 | NIV |

17. *Finally, be strong in the Lord and in his mighty power. Ephesians 6:10 | NIV |*

18. *Yours, Lord, is the greatness and the power and the glory and the majesty and the splendor, for everything in heaven and earth is yours. Yours, Lord, is the kingdom; you are exalted as head over all 1 Chronicles 29:11 | NIV |*

19. *Love the Lord your God with all your heart and with all your soul and with all your mind and with all your strength. Mark 12:30 | NIV |*

20. *Now to him who is able to do immeasurably more than all we ask or imagine, according to his power that is at work within us, to him be glory in the church and in Christ Jesus throughout all generations, forever and ever! Amen. Ephesians 3:20-21 | NIV |*

21. *So, he said to me, "This is the word of the Lord to
Zerubbabel: 'Not by might nor by power, but by
my Spirit,' says the Lord Almighty."
Zechariah 4:6 | NIV |*

22. *For who is God besides the Lord?
And who is the Rock except our God?
Psalm 18:31 | NIV |*

23. *For the message of the cross is foolishness to those
who are perishing, but to us who are being saved it
is the power of God.
1 Corinthians 1:18 | NIV |*

24. *It was not by their sword that they won the land,
nor did their arm bring them victory;
it was your right hand, your arm,
and the light of your face, for you loved them.
Psalm 44:3 | NIV |*

25. *For since the creation of the world God's invisible
qualities — his eternal power and divine nature —
have been clearly seen, being understood from
what has been made, so that people are without
excuse. Romans 1:20 | NIV |*

26. For in Christ all the fullness of the Deity lives in
bodily form, and in Christ you, have been brought
to fullness. He is the head over every power and
authority.

27. The Lord is my strength and my shield;
my heart trusts in him, and he helps me.
My heart leaps for joy,
and with my song I praise him.
Psalm 28:7 | *NIV* |

28. The Almighty is beyond our reach and exalted in
power;
in his justice and great righteousness, he does not
oppress.
Job 37:23 | *NIV* |

29. Wealth and honor come from you;
you are the ruler of all things.
In your hands are strength and power
to exalt and give strength to all.
1 Chronicles 29:12 | *NIV* |

30. Who has done this and carried it through,
calling forth the generations from the beginning?
I, the Lord – with the first of them
and with the last – I am he.
Isaiah 41:4 | *NIV* |

31. *But you will receive power when the Holy Spirit
comes on you; and you will be my witnesses in
Jerusalem, and in all Judea and Samaria, and to
the ends of the earth.*
Acts 1:8 | *NIV* |

32. *His divine power has given us everything we need
for a godly life through our knowledge of him who
called us by his own glory and goodness.*
2 Peter 1:3 | *NIV* |

33. *The Lord gives strength to his people;
the Lord blesses his people with peace.*
Psalm 29:11 | *NIV* |

34. *Though one may be overpowered,
two can defend themselves.
A cord of three strands is not quickly broken.*
Ecclesiastes 4:12 | *NIV* |

I command every adversary against your life and family broken into pieces, adversary against your marriage broken into pieces, adversary against your job broken into pieces, adversary against your greatness, against your future, broken into pieces, I command in the name of Jesus, every hand of the enemy against you broken in pieces, by fire by fire, out of heaven shall the lord rain thunder against your adversaries.

He shall judge the ends of the earth and He shall give strength unto His king, and exalt the horn of his anointed.

Make the following declarations.

I receive Jesus Christ as my personal lord and savior and declare, I am a child of God.

I receive your strength, from the crown of my head to the soul of my feet.

O Lord I am strengthened, I receive your strength, to have a right standing with you, to believe in your word and then to depend on you completely in my life.

Father let your strength be my fortress, I command every wall resisting my blessings, by the strength of God, break into pieces, I wear my shoes of Iron and Brass and I step upon the devil and I crush his head.

I wear my shoes of Iron and brass in your strength and I crush every hand of the enemy against my life, Amen!!